What Is Gravity?

Eduardo Aparicio

Contents

Rigby.

Introduction

Do you wonder why things fall? Everything falls because of **gravity.** Rain falls from dark storm clouds because of gravity.

rain falling

Bright red and gold leaves
fall from trees because of gravity.
If you drop a pencil, it falls to the
floor because of gravity.

leaves falling

Why Do Things Move?

Things don't move by themselves.
If you want a broom to sweep,
you must **push** it.

pushing a broom

4

If you want to take a friend for a ride in a wagon, you have to **pull** the wagon. The wagon won't move by itself!

Pushing and pulling are **forces** that make things move.

pulling a wagon

Why Do Things Fall?

Sometimes a thing seems to move without any force pushing or pulling it. When you throw a ball up in the air, it seems to come back down by itself. You don't have to pull it down.

What makes the ball fall back to the ground? A force that you can't see is pulling it down. This force is called gravity.

gravity pulling
a ball toward Earth

7

Try This!

Here is something you can try with a friend.

1. Get two balls that are different sizes, like a soccer ball and a baseball.

2. Stand in an open place with one ball in each hand.

3. Hold your arms straight out, away from your body. Make sure that each ball is the same height from the floor.

4. Let go of both
balls at the same
time while your
friend watches.

Did the large ball hit the floor before
the small ball? No. Size doesn't matter
because gravity has pulled both balls
down at the same time.

Is Gravity Everywhere?

We have gravity on Earth, but there's very little gravity in outer space. Astronauts who travel in space have to learn new ways to do things with almost no gravity. It must have been fun for these astronauts to bounce and float inside their spaceships. But also, it must have been hard for them to do simple things like eating. Astronauts use special trays to keep their food from floating away.

astronauts doing flips

How Important Is Gravity?

Try to imagine what your classroom would be like without gravity. Your chair wouldn't simply stay on the floor. Your paper and pencils would float in the air. Your friends would be floating everywhere! Gravity keeps people and things firmly on the ground. Without gravity, Earth's rivers and oceans would drift off into space. If we didn't have gravity, life on Earth would be very different, wouldn't it?

How Does Gravity Help?

Gravity keeps your feet on the ground when you walk or run. When you go to sleep, gravity keeps you safely in your bed.

Without gravity you would float in the air just like an astronaut in space. Gravity is a force that we all use every day.

kids walking

astronaut floating
in space

Glossary

forces   what makes objects move

gravity   the force that causes objects to move toward the center of Earth

pull   to move something toward you, using force

push   to move something away from you, using force